RUBANK EDUCATIONAL LIBRARY No. 147

VanderCook

PROGRESSIVE DUETS

FOR **Cornet or Trumpet**

(Baritone Treble Clef, French Horn, Alto, Mellophone, or Any Other Two Equal Instruments in Treble Clef.)

by H. A. VanderCook

RUBANK®

HAL•LEONARD®

Six Progressive Duets in Common Time (Meter)

I

II

III

Copyright MCMXLVIII by Rubank, Inc., Chicago, Ill.
International Copyright Secured

IV

V

VI

Six Progressive Duets in 2/4 Time (Meter)

I

II

III

IV

V

VI

Six Progressive Duets in ⁶⁄₈ Time (Meter)

I

II

III

IV

V

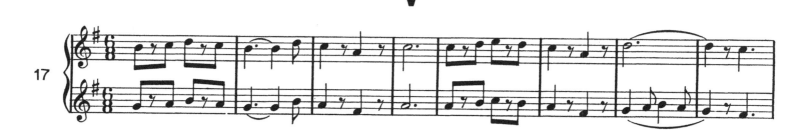

VI

Six Progressive Duets in ¾ Time (Meter)

I

II

III

IV

V

VI

Maestoso

25

Andante dolce

26

March tempo

27

Grand march

28

Allegro

29

Allo moderato

30

March tempo

31

Allegro-daintily

32

Moderato delicato

33

Spirito

34

Moderato gracile

35

Moderato

36

Con brio

37

Andantino dolce

38

Allo moderato delicato

39

Maestoso

40

Andantino dolce

41

Moderato con accento

42

1117-31

Pomposo

43

Andante

44

Andante moderato

Spirito

1117-31

Allegro risoluto

47

Andante

48

Moderato con energia

49

Allegro

50

Spirito con energia

51

Allegro

52

Allo leggiero

53

Andante and Allegro

Andante dolce

54

Allegro

Air and Variation

1117-31

Repartee

Allo moderato

Slower

Facile Duo

Allegro moderato

57

1117-31

Tête-a-Tête

Moderato (count two)

Fanfare et Marche

Grand march

1117-31

Side By Side

Tempo di Valse

60

Dance of the Fireflies